Let's Talk About
PARROTS

by Kate Morgan
illustrated by Ellis Chappell
and Guy Francis

Harcourt

Orlando   Boston   Dallas   Chicago   San Diego

Visit *The Learning Site!*
www.harcourtschool.com

Meet an Amazing and Colorful Family

Imagine this: You are walking through a dense rain forest. The sounds of monkeys, frogs, and insects echo throughout the incredible forest. You hear a screech that almost sounds like a person's voice. Looking up, you spot a red-and-yellow bird clinging to the side of a tree. The bird screeches again. You wonder, Is that parrot talking to me?

It just might be. Some members of the parrot family can actually be taught to imitate the human voice. There are approximately 340 species of brightly colored birds called parrots. They have many features in common, including large heads; curved, hooked beaks; short legs; and strong feet with two toes in front and two in back.

The Parrot Family Tree

Here are some of the more colorful members of the parrot family. Do you recognize any of them?

Scarlet Macaw

These extraordinary parrots live in the northern half of South America, in Central America, and in Mexico. Macaws were originally named by Europeans, who believed that they came from the island of Macao, near China. There are seventeen living species of macaws, which vary greatly in size. The scarlet macaw is one of the largest and most beautiful parrots, measuring three feet from its head to the tip of its tail.

Scarlet Macaw

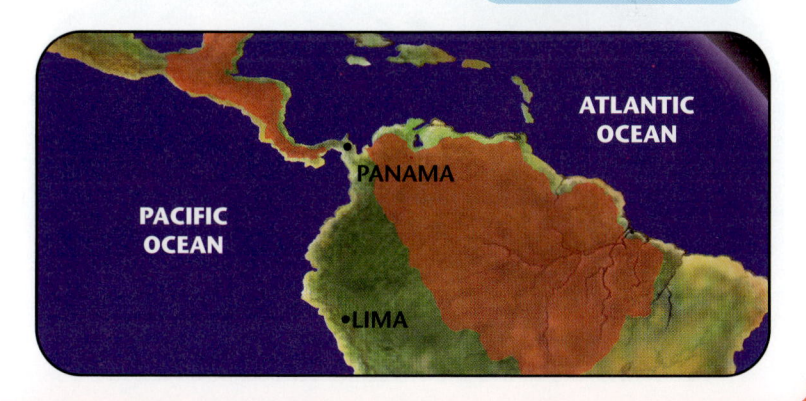

Cockatoo

These kinds of parrots are found in Australia, the East Indies, Indonesia, and the Philippines. Most of the seventeen species of cockatoo are white, although some are gray, pink, or black. They range in size from twelve to twenty inches, although the largest kind of cockatoo, the black cockatoo, can reach twenty-six inches in height. Cockatoos may live to be more than one hundred years old. Because these intelligent animals are sometimes capable of mimicking human speech, they have always been popular pet birds. They can even be taught tricks such as bowing to greet people and using their feet to "shake hands."

Cockatoo

Lovebird

Have you ever seen a pair of small parrots sitting close by each other in a cage? You might call them lovebirds. The actual species of parrots called lovebirds are found in Africa, including the island of Madagascar. Their bodies are green, blue, or yellow with red, yellow, gray, blue, or black markings on their heads. Often these birds use their tails to carry straw, grass, and sometimes even strips of paper back to their nests.

Lovebird

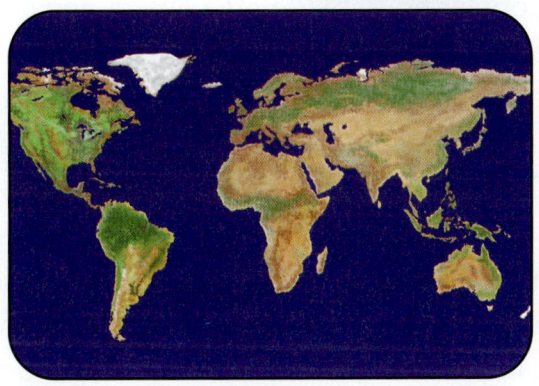

Amazon

Yellow-Headed Amazon

This amazing-looking parrot is found in the tropical rain forests of southern Mexico. Because these birds are such good "talkers," they are extremely popular as pets. In the United States, these colorful and rare birds can sell for more than one thousand dollars each.

5

Environmental

Parrots at Risk

Parrots in the wild add beauty and color to forest life. However, will they continue to survive and flourish in the tropical regions of the world?

Because they are such popular household pets, parrots have been captured and sold throughout the world. One authority has estimated that, in 1991 alone, as many as 7,500 white cockatoos were caught and sold as pets. The thick-billed parrot, found in Mexico, has also been trapped and sold as a pet or a living souvenir. This has happened despite an international agreement, signed by more than one hundred countries, that bans the buying or selling of all animals designated as endangered species.

The destruction of rain forest lands has also had a negative effect on the survival of the parrot population. When trees in the forest are cut down to make way for roads or business expansion, parrots are left without their natural habitats for nesting and feeding. To help the parrot population survive in the tropical rain forests of Peru and Bolivia, scientists have constructed nesting sites out of fake hollow trees made of plastic pipes.

Alert!

They have also cared for orphaned parrot chicks until they could reintroduce them into the wild.

What can you do to help parrots survive in the future? If you plan to buy a pet bird, vow to become an educated consumer. Ask about the origin and the breeding of the birds in that pet store. Check the bird for a closed-ring band on one of its legs. That tag means the bird is captive-bred and not imported illegally from the wilderness.

Did You Know?

- Birds are the third most popular pets in the world. Parrots make up more than 16 percent of the 50 million pet birds in the world.
- The African gray parrot can be taught to say as many as 700 words.
- Some male and female birds who are mates sing duets together. They learn each other's songs and when they are together they sing different parts. When they are apart each repeats the whole song until they are together again. Some scientists think that the reason parrots learn to talk is that they are attempting duets with their owners. By mimicking the humans who feed and care for them, they are saying, "We belong together. Let's share our sounds."

Thinking About Buying a Pet Parrot?

Parrots make wonderful pets. They are beautiful to look at, fascinating to train, entertaining to listen to, and often affectionate with their owners. Yet, before you and your family decide to buy a colorful, expensive parrot, be sure you are ready to handle the huge responsibility. The first thing to consider is a parrot's lifespan. A parrot can live to be one hundred years old. When you invite a parrot to share your home, you are making a long-term commitment! Can you picture you and your parrot when you are both eighty years old?

Parrots need daily care. They need your attention and affection. Their feathers need to be groomed. They need to be fed healthy food. Their food and water dishes need to be cleaned twice a day. Every day, seed husks and bird droppings at the bottom of their cages must be removed. Unclean cages breed bacteria and fungus that can make the birds sick.

Baby parrots need stimulating environments for the first two years of their lives. You will need to create a wonderful nursery school for your bird, with lots of interesting things to see and do. Are you ready?

10

WHAT YOU NEED
to Create a Perfect Parrot Environment

1. *One parrot.*

2. *A large safe cage* big enough for your full-grown bird to spread out its wings and turn around without touching the sides. The cage should be made of a strong metal, such as stainless steel. A bird can peck through wood or bamboo and can even rip off parts of a metal cage that are poorly constructed.

3. *A sturdy cage door latch* that a smart bird will never learn to open. A parrot that escapes can be easily injured outside its cage.

4. *Perches* for your bird to cling to inside the cage. Perches should be made of wood. Some owners make their own perches from tree branches.

5. *Lots of toys* to entertain your parrot. Choose pet store toys without sharp edges; toys with wheels, mirrors, and bells; special parrot music boxes; and take-apart toys. Make your own parrot toys using a bundle of sticks attached to the side of the cage; cloth or paper woven in and out of the cage bars; or an old pair of glasses. Parrots love chewable toys that move and make noise.

Dear Dr. Tam

Do you have questions about training your parrot to talk? Write to Dr. Tam at *Let's Talk About Parrots* and find all the answers. Dr. Lenora Tam is one of the country's leading experts on parrot behavior.

Do birds talk to each other?

All birds communicate with each other in some way. Some of these communications are instinctive and some are learned. An infant bird knows by instinct to cry out for food. Also, it can recognize the warning calls of its parents when it is born. Birds use calls to share important lifesaving information about food or danger. Many birds, usually males, sing songs to attract a mate.

How are parrots able to talk?

Parrots have a specialized organ called a syrinx located at the base of the throat. They use their thick tongues to turn the sounds made by the syrinx into human words.

My parrot ignores me. How can I get her attention?

Get as close to your bird as possible and sing as loud as you can! Your parrot will stop whatever she is doing and stare at you. She might even join in and sing a duet with you.

Help! My parrot keeps screaming! What can I do before the neighbors get upset about the commotion?

Your parrot is demanding attention! First, make sure your parrot's cage is a clean and interesting place. Next, keep a log of when the screaming occurs. For example, does your bird scream when you leave the room? Before you walk out, give it a new toy or ring its bell, so your parrot will switch its negative screaming behavior to positive playing behavior.

I just bought a three-year-old parrot. Can I still teach him to talk?

The ideal age to teach a parrot to talk is before eighteen months. Begin talking to your baby parrot in its own language. Make a sound you have heard your parrot make. When your parrot mimics that sound, praise him or her. This will become a pattern for learning human words.

The next step is to choose a short name and repeat it often. Parrots seem to have an easy time remembering names like *Polly* and *Pretty*. Once your parrot has learned its name, introduce short phrases that you would like your parrot to repeat to you, such as "Good morning" and "Hello there." Be sure to end each training session before you and your parrot become exhausted!

A Perfect Parrot Diet

1. If you eat a balanced diet, you can share it with your parrot. A parrot needs fruit, vegetables, cooked meats, and grains.

2. Figure out the right amount of food for your parrot. Your parrot needs a variety of foods in small portions. If your parrot leaves food in its dish, or drops lots of food on the floor of the cage, you are overfeeding it.

3. Give your parrot small amounts of seeds and nuts. Bird seed is not as nutritious as the food you eat.

4. Avoid bacteria and mold by removing any food your parrot does not eat.

5. Change your parrot's water twice a day. Clean the water dish more often if your parrot likes to mix food in its water.

6. Never feed your parrot coffee, kidney beans, lima beans, or avocados.

7. Do not forget tons and tons of love and attention.